10/15 LN

S0-BQX-273

Literature-Based Bulletin Boards

✦✦✦✦✦✦✦✦✦✦✦✦✦✦

Create interactive bulletin boards that turn into beautiful big books—instantly!

✦✦✦✦✦✦✦✦✦✦✦✦✦✦

by Elizabeth Shelton Wollner
and Sharon Rodgers

S C H O L A S T I C
PROFESSIONALBOOKS

New York • Toronto • London • Auckland • Sydney

Dedication

To my mother; my husband, Mark; and to all of the children at Graland
Country Day School, whose work is lovingly displayed on these pages. —*e.s.w.*

To my husband, Michael; and my children, Lauren and Ryan, with love.

And to my colleague and friend, Liz, with appreciation for the years
we shared teaching kindergarten together. —*s.r.*

Acknowledgments

Margaret Shelton Cottrell, my sister, for the writing suggestions that got me started,
for making me laugh, and for always "being there."

Susan Osgood and Beth Hower, two extraordinary friends and colleagues,
for their empathy, encouragement, and excitement.

Mona Yen Shriver, for her creative ideas and unparalleled artwork.

Carolyn Craig, for her support during our teaching year together. —*e.s.w.*

Michael Rodgers, my husband, for his compassion and sensitive guidance in all my endeavors.

Tania Foster, for her caring nature, and the magic she creates for children. —*s.r.*

Dennis Griebel, for his technological wizardry.

Marilyn Foster, for her camaraderie and photographic assistance.

Terry Cooper, Editorial Director, Scholastic Professional Books,
for discovering the possibility of writing this book.

Deborah Schecter, Senior Editor, Scholastic Professional Books,
for her insight, guidance, and editing finesse. —*e.s.w. and s.r.*

Scholastic Inc. grants teachers permission to photocopy the patterns from this book for classroom use. No other part of this publication
may be reproduced in whole or in part, or stored in a retrieval system, or transmitted in any form or by any means, electronic, mechanical, photocopying, recording, or otherwise, without permission of the publisher. For information regarding permission, write to
Scholastic Professional Books, 555 Broadway, New York, NY 10012.

Cover design by Jaime Lucero
Cover photos by Donnelly Marks
Cover art by Elizabeth Shelton Wollner's first-grade students at Graland Country Day School
Interior design by Sydney Wright
Interior illustrations by Maxie Chambliss
Interior photos by Elizabeth Shelton Wollner, Sharon Rodgers, and Marilyn Foster

ISBN 0-590-89640-7

Copyright © 1997 by Elizabeth Shelton Wollner and Sharon Rodgers
All rights reserved.
Printed in the U.S.A.

Wayne
LB
1043.58
.W65
1997

Contents

◆ Introduction ◆

How many bulletin board displays do you create each year? For most teachers, this is a challenging but important part of the job. "Dressing up" the walls of classrooms helps to create a warm and stimulating environment. Colorful displays and interesting materials help to enrich children's time in school and motivate them to learn. Yet if you are like most  of us, from time to time you wonder about the value of your displays, and you struggle to think of new and exciting approaches to this age-old tradition.

This book presents an easy format for making bulletin boards with your students and then using the same materials to create class big books that you can use over and over again. By following this "two for one" format, you can save valuable time and involve students in making bulletin boards and class big books that are meaningful to them. You'll also find that making bulletin boards is a fun and relaxing project that your whole class enjoys.

How the "Bulletin Board to Big Book" Concept Evolved

We had been making class big books based on favorite picture books with our students for many years. The children loved them and eagerly took them home to share with their families. However, we felt that the children needed more opportunities to get involved with the text before the books went home.

At the same time we were struggling to make meaningful bulletin boards that involved the students. Our "cookie cutter" boards (where all of the children made the same cut-and-paste item such as a penguin) were driving us crazy as we measured and rearranged to get them up straight, all the time worrying about that child whose penguin just didn't quite measure up to proper penguin status.

Then one day, the light went on! We realized we could use the children's big book pictures for a bulletin board display. We used the same motivational techniques but told the children that before we made the big book, we were going to display their stories and pictures on our bulletin board.

Once the bulletin board was complete, we read it together on several occasions and since the text was already familiar, the children were soon able to read the board by themselves or with a friend. Hence the concept of "reading the room" (see page 10) came alive in our classroom.

After the bulletin board had been up for several weeks, we took it down and compiled the children's work into a big book that the children took turns taking home to share with their families. The children, with our assistance, have been creating bulletin boards and big books ever since and eagerly look forward to each new literary venture.

How to Choose a Piece of Literature

As you read through this book, you will see the types of literature from which it is easy to create bulletin boards. It's helpful if one or more of these components are elements in the book or poem you choose:

◆ **Many characters** (for example, *The Relatives Came*, page 56) Children can make one of the characters directly from the story or create their own.

Georgia's frog jumped away from a seal.

◆ **Many actions** (for example, *Jump, Frog, Jump!* page 44) Children can make their own frogs jump, leap, hop, and swim from a variety of foes.

◆ **Many places** (for example, *The Jolly Postman*, page 40) Children can think of many places to send their letters.

If you are working with younger children, it's helpful to choose a story that is fairly repetitive so children can catch on to the phrase(s) you will display on the bulletin board.

How to Introduce This Concept

1 Choose a piece of literature that you particularly like and that has a repetitive phrase, for example, *Sitting in My Box* (see page 64).

2 Read the story to children for several days, emphasizing with each reading how the story becomes like a good friend or an "old favorite."

3 As children become comfortable, ask them to chime in when the repetitive parts are read.

4 Ask children if they can think of other animals, people, and objects that might go into the box. Some children may need help thinking of an animal or may prefer to name one used in the story. You can also promote brainstorming to produce a variety of ideas for anyone to adopt.

5 Invite children to innovate on the text by telling them that they are going to write their own version of the story. Have children dictate their ideas. Encourage them to phrase their contributions in complete sentences. You may wish to model some examples.

6 Put out the art media you plan to use and have each child create a picture for the new story.

7 Arrange the text and pictures on the bulletin board.

8 Demonstrate, using a pointer, how to read the board while children join in. Encourage them to read the board with a friend during the day.

9 After the board has been up for a couple of weeks, take it down and compile it into a big class book. Students will be proud of how well they can "read" this now familiar story. Tip: Before taking down the display, have students begin working on another literature piece so that you'll have another display ready to go up.

10 Send home the big book for children to share with their families.

The ideas presented here are a starting point to ignite your own spark of creativity. Have fun with students as you personalize your room!

◆ Creating the Bulletin Boards ◆

Materials and Methods

We vary the art procedures for creating the bulletin boards so that children can experience different kinds of media. However, many of the materials will work for all of the displays. For instance, if we suggest tempera paint, feel free to use watercolors, cray-pas, or any other medium that fits into your program. If we feel that a certain method is essential to the outcome or success of the board, we have specified it as such.

After children create their pictures, especially if they use paint, let the pictures dry. Then place the papers under a heavy book or big block to prevent them from curling too much. When gluing the pictures onto the pages for the class book, we recommend rubber cement because it produces the fewest wrinkles. Be sure also to place the glued-on pictures under a heavy book or block to ensure adhesion.

Lively Lettering

We usually display our titles and captions in capital and lowercase letters so children have authentic practice recognizing those letters. However, you can create the letters in many different ways. Here are a few suggestions:

◆ Hand letter, print, or use calligraphy-style lettering for the captions and titles. For fun, print block letters with a felt tip marker and add big dots at the corners or ends of each letter. Write captions on strips of colored paper or paper that has been cut into shapes such as clouds or bubbles.

◆ If you print titles and captions on a computer, you can make them any size you require. You can also enlarge print on some copy machines.

◆ You can purchase precut letters at any teacher store.

◆ Trace letter stencils onto construction paper, wallpaper, wrapping paper, metallic paper, or newspaper.

◆ To make letters look more prominent, glue the cut-out letters onto a contrasting color of paper and then cut around the letter, leaving $1/8$ inch of the contrasting color showing around the outside.

Assembling the Display

◆ To attach pictures securely to the wall, use staples or straight pins.

◆ When taking the materials off the bulletin board, use a staple remover to avoid tearing the pictures.

◆ If you are mounting your display on a wall instead of a bulletin board, try using Funtak or rolled pieces of masking tape for easy removal.

◆ Not all displays have to be on the bulletin board. Hanging materials from a clothesline strung across your room (for example, *The Important Book*, page 36) is an eye-catching way to display students' work.

◆ Compiling the Class Big Books ◆

Book Covers

◆ You can make book covers in many different shapes. Children particularly enjoy covers that are different from the usual squares or rectangles. By starting with a rectangle and adding a handle, you have a suitcase (*The Relatives Came*, page 56). If you add a triangular top, you've made a house (*Houses*, page 28).

◆ Ask one or two children to paint the picture for the cover. Give credit to the artist(s) on the inside of the cover.

◆ Use one of the children's pictures that has already been made for the book as the cover. To do this in a manner that feels fair to children, we choose a name out of a hat. When using inside art as the cover, we make a light copy of the picture and have the child color it in.

◆ We make our book covers of tagboard or poster board to ensure durability. The size and design of the cover dictate the size of the pictures students can make for the book. Keep this in mind when you give students the paper on which to make their pictures.

Title Page and Dedication Page

◆ When we compile a class big book, we try to include some of the components found in "real" books. Every published book contains a title page. On our title page, we always include the title, authors, date, and an acknowledgment of the original version from which we rewrote or adapted our version.

◆ Occasionally, the class likes to include a dedication page. A book about families might be dedicated to parents, while a book about frogs might be dedicated to the science teacher. This is a meaningful way for children to think about the importance others have in their lives.

About the Authors Page

When reading stories to the class, we often read the biographical information about the authors so that children can identify with them as real people. When we compile our own class books, we frequently include an about the authors page. Sometimes we compose the description, but often we ask children (as a whole class or in small groups) to think of information about themselves that should be included. Students may also want to draw self-portraits for this page.

Protecting Your Products

It's not necessary to laminate each page of every book. We often laminate just the front and back covers. Occasionally, however, in order to strengthen the pages, it is a good idea to laminate or cover the pages with clear adhesive contact paper.

Binding the Book

There are several methods for binding books. You can use metal O rings, which come in an assortment of sizes. Yarn, ribbon, or string woven through holes punched in the side of the book and shower curtain rings also work well. If you mount children's pictures on the fronts and backs of each page, brass paper fasteners work well. You can also purchase plastic binders if your school has a book-binding machine available.

Who Sank The Boat?

Rewritten and illustrated by First Grade

◆ Bringing Literature to Life ◆

"Reading the Room"

"Reading the room" is one of children's favorite activities. We keep a basket of eyeglass frames and several types of "reading wands" in our room. Children don the glasses and walk around the room pointing to and reading all of the print they see, especially the bulletin boards. Our reading wands are the liquid-filled sparkle plastic wands available in toy stores. For longer wands, we decorate dowel rods, available in craft or hardware stores. For safety, we glue an orange cap from an old glue bottle at the end.

Sending Literacy Home

One of the most valuable aspects of making the class big books is sending them home for children to read with their families. At the back of each book we add the parent pages, which give parents and other family members an opportunity to sign that they have read the book and to offer a comment about the story. Each time the book is returned to school, we read the comments to the class. Everyone loves hearing the wonderful things family members say.

We attach the actual trade book to the class big book so children and families can read the original version as well as the class version. Keeping them attached helps ensure the safe return of both books. If the trade book is a paperback, you can punch a hole in the book with a hole punch by inserting a few pages at a time into the punch. Place a hardcover book into a plastic bag with a hole punched in it. Attach the trade books to the class big book with a metal ring.

Book bags are essential to the safe transportation of big books between home and school. We have used commercially made bags but are more satisfied with ones we make ourselves because they better meet our size requirements. We buy the material, specify the dimensions, and ask parent volunteers to make simple tote bags with handles that children can carry. If plastic bags from department stores are used, label them clearly so they aren't accidentally thrown away.

After all children have had an opportunity to take the book home, we keep the books in our classroom library so children can reread them whenever they like. Occasionally, it is fun to lend them to another class or let children do an oral reading of the book to another class.

Literature Titles

Use this chart to see at a glance how our literature selections for bulletin board/big book projects fit your students' needs.

Titles	Pattern/ Predictable	Rhyming	Traditional Literature	People/ Families	Animal Themes	Emergent Readers	Independent Readers
At Home in the Coral Reef					x		
Band-Aids		x		x			x
The Enormous Turnip			x	x			x
The Gingerbread Man	x		x		x		
Houses				x			
I Love You, Good Night	x			x	x	x	x
The Important Book	x		x	x			x
The Jolly Postman				x			
Jump, Frog, Jump!	x				x		x
The Mitten	x		x		x		x
Peter's Pockets				x			x
The Relatives Came				x			
Rosie's Walk	x				x		
Sitting in My Box	x	x			x	x	
Ten Black Dots	x					x	
When the King Rides By	x	x		x			x
Who Sank the Boat?	x	x			x		x

At Home in the Coral Reef

by Katy Muzik and Katherine Brown
Charlesbridge, 1992

Beautiful watercolor pictures depict the variety of life on a coral reef. The thoughtful information and magnificent illustrations will attract under-the-sea lovers of all ages.

Making the Bulletin Board

Materials You Need

- ▲ white construction paper
- ▲ tempera paint and paintbrushes
- ▲ collage items such as yarn, wiggly eyes, and glitter
- ▲ blue bulletin board paper
- ▲ blue cellophane
- ▲ index cards for captions

- ▲ butcher paper
- ▲ bath sponges and bubble wrap with small air pockets
- ▲ cut-out letters for the title
- ▲ scissors
- ▲ stapler
- ▲ optional: fish netting, raffia, dried eucalyptus or other dried plants (to represent underwater plants)

Here's What to Do

1 Read the story to the class. Encourage children to talk about a variety of living things in the ocean, including coral, plants, fish, and other sea animals. Also share other books related to the topic to give children more ideas about creatures and plants that live in the sea.

2 Ask each child to think of two sea creatures or plants to paint on white construction paper for the bulletin board. Provide collage items so children can add features to their creations.

3 Help children decide what they want to call their sea creatures and write the names on small caption cards cut from index cards. We use small cards so the writing doesn't interfere with the mural.

4 Let the pictures dry and cut them out. Put them under a heavy flat object to minimize curling.

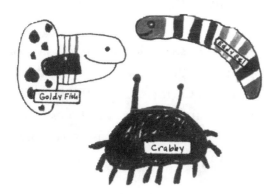

5 Cover the bulletin board with blue background paper. Cut wave scallops from blue cellophane and staple on the board.

6 Cut out large coral shapes from butcher paper. Fill in designs and patterns on the coral shapes using bath sponges and small bubble wrap. Dip the sponges into a variety of colors of tempera paint and use them to print all over the coral shapes. Use a paintbrush to cover pieces of small bubble wrap with several colors of paint. Place the bubble wrap with the paint side down on the paper and press to create an interesting design.

7 Arrange the large coral shapes on the board and staple children's sea creatures with their captions among the corals. You may wish to have children choose the place where their creature will go.

8 To enhance the ocean effect, drape fish netting along the top of the board or let it hang down from the ceiling. Place raffia and dried plants in the netting to resemble seaweed.

Making the Class Big Book

1. To capture the theme of the sea, make wavelike scallops on the book's front and back covers and inside pages. Use blue poster board for the covers and blue construction paper for the pages.

2. Carefully remove the pictures and captions from the bulletin board. Avoid tearing children's work.

3. Glue each picture with its caption on the scalloped paper. Depending on the size of students' paintings, two or more sea creatures or plants may fit on each page.

4. Cut the large coral shapes into smaller ones and use these on the front and back covers. Glue the title of the book on the front cover, using the letters from the bulletin board if they fit. Laminate the pages if desired.

5. Punch two holes in the left side of each page and assemble the book using metal O rings. Or tie the pages together using strands of raffia as you would use yarn. You can also assemble this book with plastic book binders.

Materials You Need

- ▲ blue poster board
- ▲ large blue construction paper
- ▲ metal O rings, plastic book binders, or raffia
- ▲ rubber cement or white school glue
- ▲ cut-out letters for the title
- ▲ scissors

Extending Learning

◆ MATH

Make charts of ocean-related statistics. For example, help children record the lengths of different sea creatures, or the depths of different parts of the ocean.

◆ SCIENCE

Help students research coral reef animals and plants that are named after their unique appearance (brain corals, sea lettuce, seahorses, starfish). Students can then make an illustrated poster of their creatures and share information they learned with another class.

◆ HOME-SCHOOL CONNECTION

If any parents scuba dive, ask them to come and talk with the class. Also, children often have seashells from vacations that they love to bring in to share.

◆ FIELD TRIP

If you don't live near an aquarium, check with local pet store owners. They often welcome class visits. Exotic fish await you!

◆ LITERATURE LINKS

A House for Hermit Crab by Eric Carle (Picture Book Studio, 1987)

Big Al by Andrew Clements (Scholastic, 1988)

The Magic School Bus on the Ocean Floor by Joanna Cole (Scholastic, 1992)

Swimmy by Leo Lionni (Pantheon, 1963)

STARFISH by Mia

Starfish have hundreds of tiny tiny suckers on their feet.

HERMIT CRAB by WILL

Hermit crabs live in empty shells that belonged to other animals.

Sea Sponge by Maddy

Sea Sponges live on the bottom of the ocean.

Band–Aids

from *Where the Sidewalk Ends*
by Shel Silverstein
HarperCollins, 1974

The child in this poem loves to wear Band-Aids, even if they aren't needed. *Where the Sidewalk Ends* is a collection of poems and drawings with a rich blend of warmth and wit.

Making the Bulletin Board

Materials You Need

▲ white and tan construction paper
▲ regular-size Band-Aids
▲ tempera paint and paintbrushes
▲ colorful children's Band-Aids
   (small size)

▲ 12-by-18-inch paper
▲ white correction fluid or white paint
▲ broad-tip black marker
▲ scissors
▲ stapler

Here's What to Do

1 Read the poem to the class. Ask: Why do you think the person in the poem wanted so many Band-Aids? Did the person need so many? Encourage children to share their own feelings about Band-Aids.

2 Invite children to paint pictures of themselves. After the pictures dry, guide children in cutting them out. Then give children Band-Aids to put on their pictures. (Small sizes will fit on the pictures better, and the colors will show up better on the bulletin board.)

3 Copy and enlarge the Band-Aid pattern below. Use it to trace and cut out a large Band-Aid for each child on tan construction paper. Use correction fluid or white paint (with a very fine brush) to create the "air holes" on the middle pad part of the Band-Aid. Using a broad marker, write captions generated by children on the Band-Aids. For example, *Jamie has a Band-Aid on her foot.*

4 Draw and cut out a large speech balloon for each child on white paper. Or invite children to make these themselves. Then ask children to write "OUCH!" and make some sort of design on their speech balloon. These go around the border of the bulletin board.

5 Print the poem "Band-Aids" on a sheet of 12-by-18-inch paper so the poem can be read from the board. Cut it out in an interesting shape and mount it on different-color paper. Cut around it, leaving a 1-inch border, following the same shape as the poem paper.

6 Optional: Draw a box of Band-Aids and glue a bunch of Band-Aids to give the appearance that the box has spilled and all of the Band-Aids have fallen out.

7 Staple the speech balloons around the border of the bulletin board and mount the poem and the spilled box of Band-Aids in one corner. Engage children in helping you arrange the pictures with the Band-Aid captions on the board.

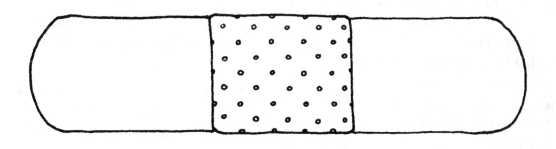

Making the Class Big Book

Materials You Need

▲ tan or light brown poster board
▲ construction paper or bulletin board paper
▲ rubber cement or school glue
▲ cut-out letters for the title
▲ metal O rings, plastic book binders, or a roll of gauze
▲ scissors

Here's What to Do

1 To go along with the theme of the poem, make a Band-Aid shaped book cover. When the book is opened all the way, the front and back covers should make a complete Band-Aid. Use tan or light brown poster board, approximately 25 inches long and 17 inches high. Use scissors to round the top and bottom corners of the right side of the board. About 6 inches from the left side, draw a curved line to represent the pad part of the Band-Aid. Dot on white paint to represent the air holes on the pad. Make the back cover in the same way.

2 If you made a spilled box of Band-Aids for the bulletin board, glue it on the front cover.

3 Cut out letters from construction paper for the title and glue them to the cover.

4 For the inside pages of the book, cut the construction paper in a rectangle to fit inside the cover.

5 Carefully remove the pictures and captions from the bulletin board using a staple remover to avoid tearing children's work.

6 Glue each picture with its captions on the inside pages. Laminate the pages if desired.

7 Punch two holes at the left side of each page and assemble the book using metal O rings. For an authentic look, after the holes are punched use gauze (rolled into a long cord) to tie the book together. This book can also be bound with plastic book binders.

Extending Learning

◆ SCIENCE

Children love to tell stories of injuries. Use this opportunity to teach a lesson on how to take care of minor cuts and what to do if you are injured. This is also an excellent time to talk about germs.

◆ MATH

Challenge children to figure out how many Band-Aids are used in the poem. How many are on the bulletin board? In the big book? In a box that you buy at the store?

◆ DRAMATIC PLAY

Invite children to role-play safety rules to minimize the chance of injuries. For example, children might demonstrate how to use scissors safely, how to hand a pencil to someone, or how to carry glass or other breakable objects. You might also take the class outside and have children act out good safety rules on the playground.

◆ LANGUAGE ARTS

Help the class memorize the poem with one or two children learning each line. Then perform it for another class. Encourage children to innovate on the text and write their own versions of the poem in mini-book form.

◆ LITERATURE LINKS

A Bad, Bad Day by Kirsten Hall (Scholastic, 1995)

Alexander and the Terrible, Horrible, No Good Very Bad Day by Judith Viorst (Scholastic, 1972)

Mean Soup by Betsy Everitt (Trumpet, 1992)

Oh Bother by Bronwen Scarffe (Multimedia International and Scholastic, 1986)

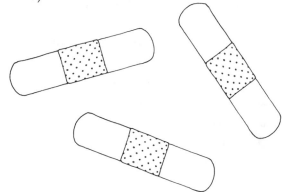

The Enormous Turnip

by Kathy Parkinson
Whitman, 1985

One of Grandfather's turnips grows to such an enormous size that the whole family including the dog, cat, and mouse try with all their might to pull it up.

Making the Bulletin Board

Materials You Need

- ▲ white, green, and purple construction paper
- ▲ tempera paint and paintbrushes
- ▲ cut-out letters for the title
- ▲ scissors
- ▲ stapler
- ▲ glue or glue stick

Here's What to Do

1. Read different versions of the story to the class. You'll find several suggestions under Literature Links on page 23.

2. Guide children in comparing various author and illustrator styles. Help them discover similarities and dif-

ferences in the stories and notice how the characters are the same or different. You might make a chart listing students' observations.

3 Have each child paint an animal or person with arms or paws outstretched as if pulling something. Work with students to come up with captions for their characters. Write each child's caption on a piece of white paper and cut around it to create a bubble shape.

4 Let the pictures dry and then cut them out.

5 Copy the turnip patterns shown below, enlarging or reducing them to make a border that will fit the size of your bulletin board. Distribute them to the class.

6 Have each child use the pattern to trace and cut out two or three turnip bottoms from purple construction paper. Then have each child trace and cut out the tops of the turnips from green construction paper. Glue the two parts together.

7 On a large sheet of purple construction paper, draw the bottom of a huge turnip and ask a child to cut it out. Draw the top of the turnip on green construction paper. Ask a child to cut it out.

8 Place the large turnip in the middle of the board and staple the pictures on the bulletin board so that the animals are pulling on one another.

9 Place children's captions near their characters.

10 Add a title to the display. Staple the small turnips around the edge of the board for the border.

Making the Class Big Book

The spider pulled the enormous turnip.

Materials You Need

▲ purple and green poster board
▲ construction paper
▲ scissors
▲ rubber cement or school glue
▲ metal O rings

Here's What to Do

1 Make two large turnips using purple poster board for the bottoms and green for the tops. (If purple or green poster board is not available, use white and paint each piece.) Glue the title to the cover. You may want to laminate these covers.

2 Carefully remove the pictures and captions from the bulletin board using a staple remover.

3 Cut the construction paper to fit inside the covers. Glue the characters and their captions on the pages.

4 Punch two holes at the top of each page and assemble the book using metal O rings.

Extending Learning

◆ SCIENCE

Students might enjoy planting turnip seeds or any other variety of seed. Record growth observations in a class book or individual journals.

◆ MATH

• If you grow plants, measure their growth weekly. Have children record the growth on wooden craft sticks.

• Children might enjoy collecting data about other record-setting vegetables. Help them find this information in books such as the *Guinness Book of World Records* and other similar resources.

◆ PHYSICAL EDUCATION

Have children participate in their own pulling event by staging a tug-of-war. Begin with evenly divided teams. Then vary the activity by having uneven numbers of children on each team, all boys and all girls on a team, a teacher on a team, etc. Discuss the results and help children draw conclusions about them.

◆ LANGUAGE ARTS

• Create a flannel board story. Encourage children to write their own versions of the story. Encourage them to think of other vegetables that might be pulled.

• Let children design a seed packet for turnips or other vegetables and write the directions for planting and care on the back.

◆ LITERATURE LINKS

There are many delightful versions of *The Enormous Turnip*. Compare and contrast these stories with the ones your class has read.

The Great Big Enormous Turnip by Aleksky Tolstoy (Scott Foresman, 1968)

The Turnip by Harriet Ziefert (Puffin, 1996)

The Turnip by Janina Domanska (Macmillan, 1969)

The Gingerbread Man

by Paul Galdone
Clarion, 1979

A freshly baked gingerbread man escapes when he is taken out of the oven only to meet his end in the jaws of a clever fox.

Making the Bulletin Board

Materials You Need

▲ bulletin board paper
▲ tempera paint and paintbrushes
▲ white construction paper

▲ scissors
▲ tape or stapler
▲ cut-out letters for the title
▲ glue
▲ optional: wiggly eyes, buttons

24

Here's What to Do

1 Read several versions of the story to the class (see Literature Links on page 27). Children will enjoy the cumulative text of this story. Encourage them to chime in on the refrain.

2 Compare the characters in the different versions. Also compare and contrast the old man and the old woman in each version.

3 Ask several children to paint the background scene (the road, clouds, tree) on a large sheet of bulletin board paper. Suggest that children work with a seasonal theme. For example, in the fall they might have colored leaves on the trees and ground.

4 Invite each child to choose a character that will chase the gingerbread man. Have children paint their characters. When the pictures are dry, provide buttons or wiggly eyes and glue so children can embellish their characters.

5 Ask a volunteer (or pick a name out of a hat) to paint a gingerbread man using an enlarged copy of the pattern shown here.

6 Let the pictures dry and cut them out. Remember to place them under a heavy object to prevent curling.

7 Invite students to write or dictate labels for each picture on a small piece of construction paper.

8 Place the pictures with their labels on the bulletin board extending the full length of the road. Have the gingerbread man running in the front.

9 Put the title on the board in a wavelike manner. Write out a speech balloon, "Run, run, as fast as you can . . ." Place it near the gingerbread man or print it going along the road.

Making the Class Big Book

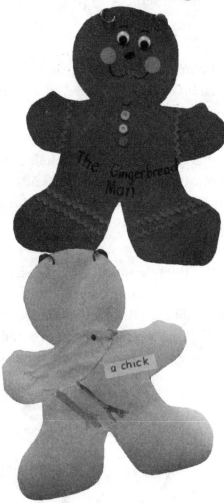

▲ brown poster board
▲ construction paper or bulletin board paper
▲ tempera paint and paintbrushes
▲ rubber cement or school glue
▲ metal O rings or brown ribbon
▲ cut-out letters for the title
▲ optional: rickrack, buttons, wiggly eyes

Here's What to Do

1 Cut the poster board into two large gingerbread man shapes for the front and back of the book. (Copy and enlarge the pattern on page 25.)

2 Decorate the cover. Ask a volunteer to paint features on the gingerbread man or add buttons, rickrack, or movable eyes for a special effect.

3 For the inside of the book, use the pattern to cut construction paper or bulletin board paper into a gingerbread shape for each child's page.

4 Print the title or glue cut-out letters on the cover of the book.

5 Carefully remove the pictures and labels from the bulletin board. Glue them on the inside pages. Laminate the pages if desired.

6 Punch two holes at the top of the cover and on each page. Assemble the book using metal O rings or tie with brown ribbons.

Extending Learning

◆ SCIENCE

#108 08-25-2009 4:58PM
Item(s) checked out to p103339097.

TITLE: Creating rooms of wonder : valuin
BARCODE: 32887925105506to1ug
DUE DATE: 09-15-09

TITLE: Language arts : interactive bulle
BARCODE: 305310012445140c4bg
DUE DATE: 09-15-09

TITLE: Literature-based bulletin boards
BARCODE: 310029021864350ak2ug
DUE DATE: 09-15-09

CCPL - Fairview Park
440-333-4700

farm
ing
hey
or
res of
gs or

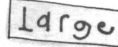

◆ MATH

Buy or make gingerbread man cookies. (If you make them in class, children will get experience measuring and counting ingredients.) Then make gingerbread man graphs: Pass out the gingerbread man cookies and have each child take a bite. Make a graph showing which part each child eats first: arm, leg, or head. If children eat the whole cookie in one bite, include that data on the graph as well.

◆ DRAMATIC PLAY

Help children review the story with this activity. Take the class outside and draw a road in chalk on the playground. Have children act out the chase of the gingerbread man.

◆ HOME SCHOOL CONNECTION

Send home a recipe for gingerbread cookies. Invite families to make the cookies together. You might also suggest that families take note of what part each person eats first and have children retell the story as part of the cooking event.

◆ LITERATURE LINKS

Children will enjoy reading the many versions of this story. Compare and contrast the plot, setting, characters, and endings in each version.

The Gingerbread Man by Eric A. Kimmel (Holiday House, 1993)

The Gingerbread Man: An Old English Folktale illustrated by John A. Rowe (North-South Books, 1996)

The Pancake Boy retold and illustrated by Lorinda Bryan Cauley (Putnam, 1988)

The Stinky Cheese Man by Jon Scieszka and Lane Smith (Viking, 1993)

Houses

by Katherine Carter
Children's Press, 1982

The photos in this book of actual houses around the world will inspire children to think about their own homes.

Making the Bulletin Board

Materials You Need

- ▲ white and black construction paper
- ▲ wallpaper samples (old wallpaper books can be obtained from paint stores)
- ▲ yellow tempera paint and paintbrushes
- ▲ cut-out letters for the title
- ▲ scissors
- ▲ stapler

28

Here's What to Do

1. With the class, read the story and share the pictures. Call attention to the many kinds of houses in the world. Point out that many people live in homes that are not houses. Give examples such as trailers or apartment buildings. Ask children to name things that make a house a home.

2. Encourage children to think of special things about their own homes. If children name material possessions, help them focus on the nonmaterial aspects of a home as well.

3. Using pieces of wallpaper samples and glue, ask children to make a picture that represents their home. Talk about how they might use the colors and patterns in the wallpaper to represent the colors and designs in their homes. Some children may need additional suggestions or help, but don't jump in too early.

4. Place children's pictures under a heavy object to ensure that the glue sticks well. Cut out the homes when they are dry.

5. Have children write or dictate three (or more) things that are special about their home.

6. Choose one or two children to make a picture of your school for the center of the bulletin board.

7. Cut black construction paper into 4-inch-wide strips that are long enough to make a street running "north and south" and one running "east and west" on the board. Paint a yellow dotted line down the middle of each strip so that it looks like a street.

8. Cut the letters for the title out of wallpaper.

9. Staple the streets on the bulletin board so that they cross in the middle and there are four sections for houses. Put the school in the middle of the street intersection.

10. If you know which students live north, south, east, and west of the school, you might place their homes and captions in similar locations on the bulletin board "map."

Making the Class Big Book

1 Make the cover into a shape of a house using black and red poster board. Cut a rectangle for the house out of a piece of 12-by-18-inch black poster board. Cut a triangle for the roof out of red poster board, making the base 18 inches long. Tape the red roof to the black house using clear tape. Reinforce the seam with an additional strip of red poster board on the back.

2 Glue the title letters on the cover. Laminate or cover the book with contact paper to make it more sturdy.

3 For the inside pages, cut construction paper into house shapes.

4 Carefully remove the pictures and captions from the bulletin board using a staple remover to avoid tearing children's work.

5 Glue the road strips along the bottom of each page so that it looks as if the road is running through the book.

6 Glue children's pictures on each page. You might also want to include a photograph of each child at

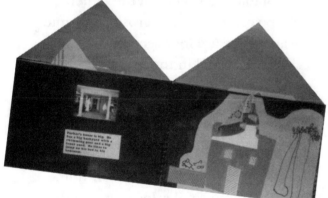

Materials You Need

- ▲ black and red poster board
- ▲ construction paper
- ▲ rubber cement or school glue
- ▲ cut-out letters for the title
- ▲ metal O rings, yarn, or plastic book binders
- ▲ 2-inch-wide clear tape

his or her home. Laminate the pages if you like. (Photographs can be laminated without damaging them.)

7 Punch three holes at the left side of each page (on the house part, not the roof part) and assemble with metal O rings or yarn.

Extending Learning

◆ SOCIAL STUDIES

• Discuss building materials that are used around the world for homes and how these homes meet the needs of the people living there. You may want to have on hand appropriate resource books so children can see what various homes look like. As a follow-up, ask children to find out what their houses are made of.

• If possible, take the class on a field trip to visit a nearby building site. Arrange beforehand for the contractor to talk with children and answer their questions.

◆ ART

Invite children to construct 3-D models of their homes. Provide empty cereal boxes, small gift boxes, paper towel and bathroom tissue tubes, paint and paintbrushes, glue, and tape. Afterward, encourage children to share with classmates how they made their constructions.

◆ MATH

Ask children to estimate how many windows are in their homes. Have them count windows and make a graph or add up all the windows together. You might also collect data and make graphs showing the number of drawers, lights, doorknobs, or other common things in children's homes.

◆ LANGUAGE ARTS

Review with the class the names of different rooms in a home. Discuss which rooms children and other family members spend the most time in. Then have children write or dictate sentences about the room they consider the most important. Ask them to give reasons.

◆ LITERATURE LINKS

A House Is a House for Me by Mary Ann Hoberman (Viking, 1978)

Building a House by Byron Barton (Trumpet, 1990)

Houses and Homes by Ann Morris (Lothrop, Lee & Shepard, 1992)

How a House Is Built by Gail Gibbons (Holiday House 1990)

This Is the Place for Me by Joanna Cole (Scholastic 1991)

I Love You, Good Night

by Jon Buller and Susan Schade
Simon & Schuster, 1988

A series of tender exchanges between a mother and child make this a wonderful little book to share at a quiet time.

Making the Bulletin Board

Materials You Need

▲ white, red, and blue construction paper

▲ tempera paint and paintbrushes

▲ cut-out letters for the title

▲ scissors

▲ stapler

▲ optional: silver paper for stars

Here's What to Do

1 Read the story to the class. Call attention to the sentence "I love you like _____ loves _____." Talk about how often two things are associated and go together. Give several examples, such as *I love you like bees love honey* and *I love you like plants love the sun*. Encourage children to make up their own examples.

2 Help children decide on two things they are going to illustrate.

3 Set up paints and white construction paper at the easel or table for children to paint their pictures. Let the pictures dry and then cut them out.

4 Print the statements that go with children's pictures on white paper. Cut around them in a bubble shape. Provide a variety of sizes of heart patterns so that children can race and cut out hearts to surround their captions.

5 For the title, use red construction paper letters for "I Love You" and blue construction paper letters for "Good Night." You can also make the word "Love" out of small hearts attached to one another. Add hearts and stars around the title if desired. Place the title in the middle of the bulletin board.

6 Have children work out a plan for arranging the pictures around the title on the bulletin board.

Making the Class Big Book

1. Make two large hearts out of red poster board for the front and back covers. Add red and pink hearts all the way around the cover as you did for the captions on the bulletin board.

2. Cut the inside pages in the same heart shape as the cover. Glue children's pictures and captions on the heart-shaped paper. Laminate the pages if desired.

3. Punch two holes at the top of each page and assemble the book using metal O rings.

Extending Learning

◆ MATH

• Talk about different expressions that describe types of measurement, such as "high as the sky," that could be used to tell how much you love someone. Provide construction paper frames that children can fill in such as: *My love for you is as big as a _____. My love will last as long as _____.*

Materials You Need

▲ red and pink poster board
▲ construction paper
▲ scissors
▲ rubber cement or school glue
▲ metal O rings

- Bring candy conversation hearts to class and have children sort them by color or message. Follow up by making a graph.

◆ ART

For Valentine's Day, help children explore the color red. Provide old magazines, paint color cards from paint stores, wallpaper samples, clothing catalogs, and so on. Ask children to cut or tear out samples of the color red. Then ask: How are the reds the same? How are they different? Help children group the samples by varying shades (red-orange, pinkish-red, dark red). Then invite them to make heart-shaped collages by gluing their color samples onto construction paper.

◆ LANGUAGE ARTS

- Print several songs or pocket chart poetry about love or Valentine's Day and sing or chant them, encouraging children to point to the words.

- Discuss with children different ways that people show they care about one another. For example, helping someone, preparing special foods, running errands, doing things together. Have children think of something they might do for someone else such as a family member, friend, or neighbor. Have each child dictate his or her idea in the form of a promise to present to someone. For example, *I promise to clear the dinner dishes after supper tonight. I promise to share my toys with my brother.*

◆ LITERATURE LINKS

A Valentine for You by Wendy Watson (Houghton Mifflin, 1993)

Guess How Much I Love You by Sam McBratney (Scholastic, 1996)

Love Notes by Kate Buckley (Albert Whitman, 1988)

The Runaway Bunny by Margaret Wise Brown (Harper, 1974)

The Important Book

by Margaret Wise Brown
Harper, 1949

What makes everyday things important? Your class might be surprised by the answers. This attribute book encourages young readers to "see" with a new perspective.

Making the Bulletin Board

Materials You Need

▲ a variety of paper in different skin tones

▲ mirror
▲ crayons and markers
▲ clothesline and clothespins
▲ optional: photo of each child

Here's What to Do

1 This is a wonderful classic, and children respond positively to the repetition of the text. After reading and sharing the book, talk about the pattern of the text. Draw children's attention to how each page has three sentences of description, and the last sentence repeats the first.

2 Ask each child to choose a piece of skin-colored paper. Discuss the fact that the color of paper can never be as rich as real skin tones, but this paper represents the wonderful skin colors in the class. Provide patterns of a simple head and shoulders shape that children can trace and cut out.

3 Provide a mirror so children can look at their faces. Talk about the placement of eyes, nose, and mouth.

4 Using markers and crayons, have children draw their faces on the cut-out head and shoulders shape.

5 Ask children to think about the important things about themselves. Provide a copy of this phrase for each child. *The important thing about _____ is that he/she _____. Two other important things about _____ are that he/she _____ and _____. But the important thing about _____ is that he/she _____.* You might have children work with partners to complete the descriptions of themselves. Also have an example ready and model how you would complete a page about yourself.

6 Glue children's descriptions on the back of their pictures.

7 Consider adding a photograph of each child under the text.

8 Draw a picture or ask a child to draw a picture of a face on an extra head and shoulders cutout. Hand letter the title, "The Important Kids," along the smile on this face.

9 Laminate each page if you like. (Lamination does not damage the photographs.)

10 To display the finished work, extend a clothesline in your classroom and hang the pictures with clothespins, starting with the title page.

37

Making the Class Big Book

Here's What to Do

1 Take the pictures down and punch three holes on the left side of each one.

2 Mount the title page on a piece of poster board and cut out the head and shoulders shape. Cut a second piece for the back cover.

3 Assemble the pages with metal O rings.

Extending Learning

◆ LANGUAGE ARTS

Children might write name poems for a partner. Give an example by writing a name vertically on the chalkboard. Explain that the first word in each line of the poem begins with a letter in the name. A name poem doesn't have to rhyme. You might use this example for Debby:

Daring and bold,
Easy to get along with,
Bright and cheerful,
Best friend,
You'd like her!

Materials You Need

▲ two pieces of 12-by-18-inch poster board

▲ metal O rings

38

◆ SOCIAL STUDIES

- This book lends itself to rich discussions of values. You might begin by discussing the different things that children have already identified about themselves as being important. From there, you might compile a class list of special qualities that make people important. Follow up by providing easy-to-read biographies of famous people and help children recognize what made these people important.

- Set aside a few minutes each day to celebrate a different child's importance. You might begin by reading what the child wrote and then invite classmates to give other reasons. Vary the celebrations with songs, poems, and cards. You might also provide a special hat or button for the child to wear.

◆ HOME SCHOOL CONNECTION

Make copies of what children write about themselves and save them for the next parent visiting night. Encourage parents to write notes to their children giving additional reasons why they are important.

◆ LITERATURE LINKS

Mr. Griggs' Work by Cynthia Rylant (Orchard, 1989)

The Lorax by Dr. Seuss (Random House, 1971)

Miss Rumphius by Barbara Cooney (Viking, 1982)

The Jolly Postman

by Janet Ahlberg and Allan Ahlberg
Little, Brown, 1986

This delightful rhyming story tells how the Jolly Postman goes from house to house delivering letters to several famous fairy tale characters.

Making the Bulletin Board

Materials You Need

▲ white construction paper
▲ 5-by-7-inch white paper
▲ tempera paint and paintbrushes

▲ scissors
▲ stapler
▲ markers or crayons
▲ glue

Here's What to Do

1 Read the story to the class. Stress the rhyming nature of the text and encourage children to learn the opening lines. Discuss why people write letters and ask to whom or from whom children have written or received mail.

2 Invite children to think of characters in storybooks, in movies, or on television. Ask children to choose a character and write a letter to that character. Younger children might dictate their letters.

3 Give each child a piece of 5-by-7-inch paper with which to make personal stationery. Children might decorate the border with markers or make fancy initials at the top.

4 On a separate piece of paper, ask children to paint a picture of the character to whom they are writing.

5 Choose one child (or ask for a volunteer) to make a picture of the Jolly Postman on his bicycle.

6 Let the pictures dry and cut them out. Remember to put a heavy flat object on top of the pictures to minimize curling.

7 Copy and enlarge the postage stamp pattern below. Give each child a copy. Ask children to design stamps using crayons or markers.

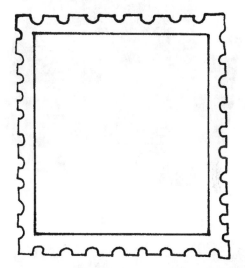

8 Staple the stamps around the edge of the bulletin board to make a border.

9 Make a picture of a mailbox. Print the book title on it.

10 Print the opening text of the book on a 5-by-7-inch piece of paper. Mount it on a colorful border.

11 Place the Jolly Postman picture, the mailbox with the book title, and the opening text in one corner of the board.

12 Enlist children's ideas about arranging the characters and letters on the board.

Making the Class Big Book

Materials You Need

▲ colored tagboard
▲ white or manila envelopes, 9-by-12-inch or larger, one per character
▲ rubber cement or school glue
▲ scissors
▲ damp sponge
▲ string or tape
▲ metal O rings or plastic book binders

Here's What to Do

1 Cut two rectangular pieces of tagboard a little larger than the 9-by-12-inch envelopes. These will be the covers of the book.

2 Carefully remove the pictures and letters from the bulletin board.

3 Glue the picture of the mailbox with the title on the front cover.

4 Glue the Jolly Postman's picture and the beginning text on the first page.

5 The envelopes will be the inside pages of the book. (Tip: Remove the sticky substance from each envelope by wetting with a damp sponge and wiping the glue off. If you leave the glue on, someone will not be able to resist the temptation of licking the envelopes and sealing them!) On the outside of each envelope, glue one of the children's characters. Place the letter to that character inside the envelope. Ask the child to "address" the envelope with the character's name. Attach each letter to its envelope with string or tape to help ensure that no letters get lost. (If you are using manila envelopes, be sure that the openings are on the right side.)

6 Glue children's postage stamps on the inside of the front and back covers to make end papers. Laminate the pages if you like.

7 Punch two or three holes at the left side of each page and assemble the book using metal O rings or plastic book binders.

Extending Learning

◆ SOCIAL STUDIES

• Arrange a visit to your local post office. Beforehand, have children prepare questions to ask. As an alternative, you might invite a mail carrier to visit your class and talk to the children.

• Study stamps from the United States and other countries. Find out if anyone's parent is a stamp collector and invite him or her to talk to the class about this hobby.

◆ MATH

Bring in stamps worth different amounts. Use a postage scale to weigh items and figure postage costs for different envelopes. Older children might figure out how much it would cost if each person in the class sends a first-class letter.

◆ DRAMATIC PLAY

Set up a post office in your classroom. Provide old envelopes, stickers, different kinds of paper, and a variety of pens and let children write, mail, and deliver letters to one another.

◆ LANGUAGE ARTS

Encourage children to write letters to real people (authors of children's books, political figures, family members). You might also set up a pen pal program with a class in another state or country.

◆ LITERATURE LINKS

Dear Annie by Judith Caseley (Greenwillow, 1991)

Dear Mr. Blueberry by Simon James (Macmillan, 1991)

Dear Brother by Frank Asch and Vladimir Vagin (Scholastic, 1992)

The Jolly Christmas Postman by Janet Ahlberg and Allan Ahlberg (Little, Brown, 1991)

Jump, Frog, Jump!

by Robert Kalan
Greenwillow, 1995

In this cumulative sequence story, a frog narrowly escapes
from a fish, snake, turtle, and children.

Making the Bulletin Board

Materials You Need

▲ tempera paint, including various
   shades of green, and paintbrushes

▲ green construction paper
▲ cut-out letters for the title
▲ straight pins
▲ stapler

44

Here's What to Do

1 Read the story to the class. Point out the repetition of the phrase "Jump, Frog, Jump" and encourage children to predict when it will occur and to join in repeating it. Point out the accumulation of events and let children try to repeat the sequence as it occurs in the story.

2 Name all of the animals in the book from which the frog jumps away. Encourage children to think of another situation or character from which the frog might have to jump.

3 Have children create frogs using tempera paint and or various shades of green construction paper. Provide paper that is no larger then 12-by-18-inches or the frogs will be too big for the class book.

4 Have each child make a lily pad from green paper. Be sure that these are large enough to include a caption.

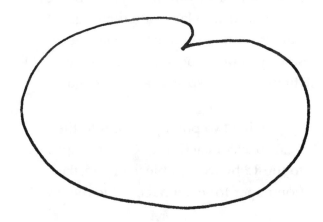

5 Write children's captions on the lily pads. For example, *Manuel's frog jumped away from _____.*

6 Arrange the title in the middle of the board, placing the letters in an up-and-down arrangement. You can staple the letters on the board or use straight pins to hold the letters out from the board to create a jumpy effect.

7 Use straight pins to attach the frogs to the board. Put the pin through the frog and push the pin into the board. Pull the frog forward, away from the board, while keeping the pin stuck in the board. Vary the parts of the frogs that are pulled away from the board to give each frog a unique jumping style.

8 Staple each lily pad close to the frog to which it belongs.

Making the Class Big Book

Materials You Need

- ▲ green tagboard
- ▲ 12-by-18-inch white construction paper
- ▲ 1-by-12-inch strips of construction paper, four per child
- ▲ school glue or rubber cement
- ▲ cut-out letters for the title
- ▲ metal O rings

Here's What to Do

1. Cut the tagboard into two 12-by-18-inch rectangles for the front and back of the book. Glue the letters on the cover in an up-and-down fashion. Laminate the cover if you like.

2. Using two of the 1-by-12-inch strips, show children how to make a pop-up spring by folding the two strips back and forth over each other. Each child will need to make two pop-up springs.

3. Carefully remove the pictures and captions from the bulletin board. You may wish to laminate the frogs before putting them in the class book since you won't be able to laminate them after the springs are attached.

4. Glue two pop-up springs to the back of each frog. Glue the springs to the 12-by-18-inch piece of construction paper for each page. Glue the lily

46

pad caption on the page with the frog. When the glue is dry, the frogs pop up as the pages are turned.

5 Punch two holes at the left side of each page and assemble the book using metal O rings.

Extending Learning

◆ SCIENCE

The life cycle study of frogs and toads is fascinating to young children. "Grow a frog" kits are available from educational and toy stores, or you could plan a trip to a local pond in the spring and catch tadpoles. As a comparison, you might investigate how other animals move.

◆ MATH

Frogs are good at jumping far. How far can children jump? Help them measure the distance using a yardstick and tape.

◆ DRAMATIC PLAY

Invite children to jump like frogs, while making frog sound effects. You might also play leapfrog on the playground. For more fun, act out the original story and add more characters.

◆ LANGUAGE ARTS

Encourage children to innovate on the text and write their own versions of the story in mini-book form.

◆ LITERATURE LINKS

Bullfrog Builds a House by Rosamond Dauer (Greenwillow, 1977)

The Frog and Toad Treasury by Arnold Lobel (HarperCollins, 1970)

Frog in the Middle by Susanna Gretz (Four Winds, 1991)

Hop, Jump by Ellen Stoll Walsh (Harcourt Brace, 1993)

In the Middle of the Puddle by Mike Thayer (HarperCollins, 1988)

The Mitten

A Ukrainian Folktale
by Jan Brett
Putnam, 1990

When Nicki drops one of his new white mittens in the snow, he doesn't even notice it's missing. One by one, the woodland animals discover the mitten and crawl inside.

Making the Bulletin Board

Materials You Need

▲ white construction paper
▲ tempera paint and paintbrushes
▲ index cards

▲ bulletin board paper
▲ cut-out letters for the title
▲ scissors
▲ stapler
▲ cotton balls

48

Here's What to Do

1 Read the story to the class. Encourage children to listen for the alliteration in the animals' names.

2 Besides the animals in the story, what other animals do children know? Ask each child to choose an animal to paint. Provide paints and paintbrushes.

3 Help children decide on names for their animals. Record these on index cards. You might ask children to think of names that begin with the same letter as the animal, for example, Benny Beaver or Taneesha Tiger. Older children might think of action words that also start with the letter of the animal. For example: *Andy Aardvark ambles into the mitten.*

4 Let the pictures dry and have children cut them out.

5 Cut out a large mitten shape from bulletin board paper. Have children glue cotton balls on the edge to look like fur. Staple the mitten in the middle of the board. Staple the cut out letters for the title on the mitten.

6 Invite children to place the animals on the board so that some animals appear to be going into the mitten. Staple the captions near the pictures.

7 Copy and enlarge the mitten pattern below for each student. Ask children to each cut out and color two or three mittens. Invite them to paint colorful patterns on their mittens. Put these around the edge of the bulletin board for the border.

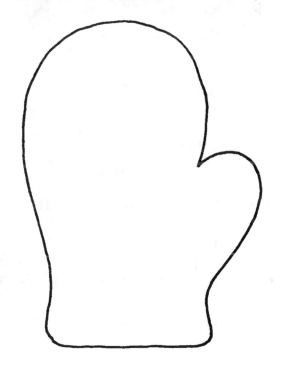

Making the Class Big Book

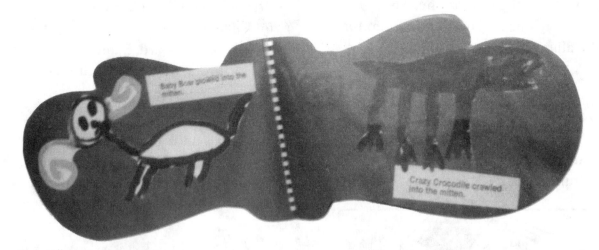

The Mitten

A Ukranian Folktale

Rewritten and illustrated
by East Kindergarten

Materials You Need

▲ two 22-by-28-inch pieces of colored
poster board

▲ construction paper or bulletin
board paper

▲ rubber cement or white school glue

▲ cut-out letters for the title

▲ metal O rings or plastic book
binders

Here's What to Do

1 Cut out two mittens from the
poster board for the front and
back covers. Pull off some of the
cotton balls from the big mitten on the
bulletin board and glue these on the
cover of the book.

2 Cut the construction paper or bulletin board paper into the same
mitten shape as the covers.

3 Take children's pictures and captions off the bulletin board using a
staple remover.

4 Glue each picture with its caption
on the inside mitten-shaped pages.
Place the glued-on pictures under a
heavy object to make sure they stick.
Laminate the pages if you like.

5 Punch three holes at the left side of each page and assemble with metal O rings or bind with plastic book binders.

Extending Learning

◆ SCIENCE

• Study animals in winter. Have children find out how different creatures survive during winter months.

• Provide examples of various animal tracks for children to identify.

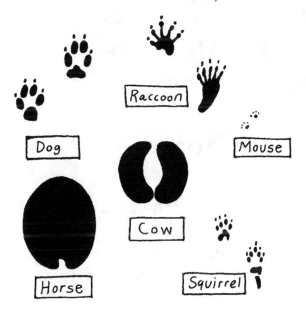

Raccoon

Dog

Mouse

Cow

Horse

Squirrel

◆ MATH

• Count the number of animals in the mitten. Count the number of legs, tails, and eyes.

• Have children bring in pairs of mittens. They can practice counting by 2s, learning left and right, making matches, or sorting by different attributes.

◆ DRAMATIC PLAY

This is a good story to dramatize. Invite children to act out their characters going into a mitten. Children might also make stick puppets to reenact the story.

◆ LANGUAGE ARTS

Encourage children to create concrete poems about mittens. Explain that a concrete poem is written in the shape of its subject. This kind of poem does not usually rhyme. For this activity, you might provide children with a mitten pattern. They can write or dictate a poem to follow the mitten outline or fill in the mitten with their poem.

◆ LITERATURE LINKS

Bring in several other versions of the story. Compare and contrast them. Here are some wonderful ones.

Any Room for Me? by Leok Koopmans (Floris Books, 1990)

The Mitten by Alvin Tresselt (Lothrop, Lee & Shepard, 1964)

The Old Man's Mitten by Yvonne Pollock (Multimedia International and Scholastic, 1986)

Peter's Pockets

by Eve Rice
Greenwillow, 1989

Peter's new pants don't have any pockets, so Uncle Nick lets Peter use his until
Peter's mother solves the problem in a clever and colorful way.

Making the Bulletin Board

Materials You Need

- ▲ construction paper
- ▲ two pieces of white poster board
- ▲ tempera paint and paintbrushes
- ▲ cut-out letters for the title
- ▲ scissors
- ▲ stapler or thumbtacks
- ▲ paste, glue, or glue stick
- ▲ optional: buttons, lace, old zippers, old buckles

Here's What to Do

The day before you read the story, ask children to think about pockets. Where do they have pockets? What do they use them for? If you are going to do the math extension (see page 54), encourage children to wear clothes with pockets the next day.

2 Read the story to the class. After-ward, discuss the variety of pockets in the story. Discuss the things that Peter collected. Ask if anyone has something in a pocket now. Make a list of things that children have in their pockets.

3 Model for children how to make a paper pocket. Fold a piece of con-struction paper in half and cut off the bottom open edges at an angle as shown.

4 Ask children to paint the outside of their pocket to look like a favorite article of clothing the pocket might go on.

5 Let the paint dry and put the pock-ets under a heavy object to keep them flat. Provide glue and buttons, lace, old zippers, etc., for children to embell-ish their pockets if they wish.

6 Encourage children to think of something they would like to have in their pocket. Provide a variety of colors of construction paper and ask children to make and cut out things to put in their pockets. Have children glue their items to the inside page of their pockets. Let the glue dry.

7 Write two captions for each child's pocket. The caption on the front tells what article of clothing this pocket is on. For example: *This is the pocket from Hiroshi's swimming suit.* The second cap-tion on the inside page tells what is in the pocket. For example: *There is a starfish and a clam in his pocket.*

8 Make two pockets from white poster board just like the ones children used. Glue cut-out letters for the title on the front of one white pock-et. On the inside of this pocket, print the author page. When you take the pockets off the bulletin board, these will make the front and back covers of the class book.

9 Laminate the pages before putting them on the board since children will be lifting the flaps to read each of the pockets.

10 Ask children to help you arrange the pockets on the bulletin board. Use staples or thumb-tacks to attach the back page of each pocket to the board so that the front flap can be lifted.

11 Give each child two or three small pockets to decorate and cut out. Staple these around the edge of the display to create a border.

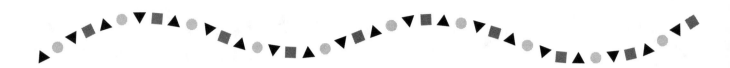

Making the Class Big Book

He has a helicopter in his pocket.

Materials You Need

▲ hole punch
▲ metal O rings

Here's What to Do

1 Remove the paper pockets and the poster board pockets from the bulletin board.

2 Punch two holes at the top of each paper pocket and assemble between the poster board pockets using metal O rings.

Extending Learning

◆ **MATH**

• Have children record the number of pockets in the classroom. They can also investigate questions such as: Are there more items of clothing with pockets or without pockets? What is the average number of pockets an item of clothing has? Do more girls or boys have pockets?

• Let each child grab a handful of pennies or buttons to put in a pocket. Have a partner estimate how many items are in the pocket. Children can then remove the items and count them. Help children record their estimates and results on a class chart.

◆ **ART**

Invite children to sew real pockets. Provide each child with two pieces of felt cut into a pocket shape, a thick needle, and embroidery thread. Model how to sew running stitches around three sides, leaving the top open.

◆ SOCIAL STUDIES

Use the theme of pockets to help children relate the jobs people do to the tools they use. For example, you might say: I am a carpenter. What tool might I carry in my special carpenter pocket? Other jobs to ask about include plumber, artist, writer, cook, teacher, doctor.

◆ LANGUAGE ARTS

Provide envelopes for children to use as pockets. Tell them to draw a picture of something to place in their pocket. On the outside of the envelope, children write clues about what is inside. The rest of the class reads the clues and tries to guess what the pocket contains.

◆ LITERATURE LINKS

A Pocket for Corduroy by Don Freeman (Viking, 1978)

Katy No-Pocket by Emmy Payne (Scholastic, 1994)

"Keep a Poem in Your Pocket" by Beatrice Schenk DeRegniers, in *The Random House Book of Poetry for Children* edited by Jack Prelutsky (Random House, 1983)

More Magic in Your Pockets by Bill Severn (McKay, 1980)

The Relatives Came

by Cynthia Rylant
Simon & Schuster, 1985

What a visit! All those relatives from Virginia have piled into their car and driven north to visit. During their stay there is much hugging, eating, working, and playing.

Making the Bulletin Board

Materials You Need

- ▲ white construction paper
- ▲ tempera paint and paintbrushes
- ▲ cut-out letters for the title
- ▲ scissors
- ▲ stapler
- ▲ optional: wallpaper or wrapping paper scraps and glue

Here's What to Do

1 Read the story to the class. As children respond to this rollicking tale, encourage them to share their own stories about favorite relatives or family gatherings.

2 Ask children to choose a favorite relative and to think of something that person likes to do. Remind children that the relative can be someone who lives at home with them.

3 At the art table, have children paint their relatives. Encourage children to use wallpaper pieces to make clothes if they wish. (When parents see the picture their child made, it is common to hear comments such as, "That looks just like Grandma Marge." At the end of the year, parents often request to have the page with their family member's picture.)

4 Print the captions for each child's relative. For example: *Grandma Marge likes to talk.*

5 Choose one child or ask for a volunteer to paint a picture of the station wagon loaded down with suitcases.

6 Let the pictures dry and have children cut them out. Remember to place the dry paintings under a large flat object to minimize curling.

7 Staple the cut-out letters for the title and the station wagon on the bulletin board.

8 Ask children where they would like their pictures to be placed. Have them help you complete the display.

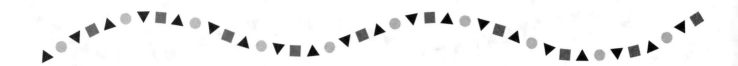

Making the Class Big Book

1. Make the book covers in the shape of a suitcase. (Our suitcase needed to be more vertical than horizontal since most of the children painted their relatives taller than wider.) Using 18-by-22-inch poster board, determine what size your suitcase needs to be. Then cut a handle at the top and round the corners. For an authentic look, get a luggage tag from an airline and attach it to the handle.

2. For the inside pages of the book, cut the construction paper for each child's page in a rectangle to fit inside the cover.

3. Carefully remove the pictures and captions from the bulletin board using a staple remover to avoid tearing children's work.

4. Glue the station wagon on the cover with the cut-out letters of the title.

5. Glue one picture with its caption on each page. To save paper, you might want to glue the pictures using the front and back of each page. If you do this, be aware that if you laminate the

Materials You Need

▲ two pieces of 18-by-22-inch brown poster board
▲ large construction paper or bulletin board paper
▲ scissors
▲ rubber cement or white school glue
▲ cut-out title letters from the board
▲ metal O rings or plastic binders
▲ optional: luggage tag

pages, sometimes the outline of the picture on the other side shows through.

6 Punch three holes at the left side of each page and assemble the book using metal O rings or plastic book binders.

Extending Learning

◆ SOCIAL STUDIES

This story lends itself to wonderful discussions of families, cultures, and traditions and brings out the humorous as well as the affectionate aspects of relationships. Find out what countries are represented by the children in your class and locate those countries on a map or globe.

◆ MATH

Count how many relatives are in each illustration in the story. Count by 2s to find out how many arms, legs, and eyes there are.

◆ LANGUAGE ARTS

Use this opportunity to review words for family members. Start with familiar words such as *mother, father, brother, sister, aunt, uncle, cousin, grandmother,* *grandfather.* Discuss variations of these words such as *mom, ma, mama, mommy.* If any children speak another language, encourage them to give the words for these names in that language. Make a chart of family words in different languages.

◆ HOME-SCHOOL CONNECTION

Send home a letter asking for favorite family recipes. Compile these into a class cookbook. If you can make multiple copies, this makes a great gift to send home at the end of the school year. You might also ask parents to send in samples of some of the recipes for the class to taste.

◆ LITERATURE LINKS

Amelia Bedelia's Family Album by Peggy Parish (Avon Books, 1989)

Fathers, Mothers, Sisters, Brothers: A Collection of Family Poems by Mary Ann Hoberman (Scholastic, 1991)

Knock! Knock! by Jackie Carter, (Scholastic, 1993)

What Is a Family? by Gretchen Super (Troll, 1991)

Rosie's Walk

by Pat Hutchins
Simon & Schuster, 1968

In this amusing story, Rosie the hen goes for a walk and inadvertently foils successive attempts on her life by a predatory fox.

Making the Bulletin Board

Materials You Need

▲ white and red construction paper

▲ tempera paint and paintbrushes

▲ scissors

▲ stapler

▲ optional: class picture

Here's What to Do

1 Read the story to the class. Encourage children to respond to the predicaments in which the fox finds himself. Discuss the prepositions used in the story and the places Rosie walks.

2 Go on a walk around your school. Explore different prepositions by having children actually go *down* the slide or *through* the door. Record the places where the class walks. Help children remember where they've been by pointing out attributes such as a shiny slide, hard blacktop, number of steps, etc.

3 Retell your own story back in the classroom, emphasizing each place children walked. Help children decide which place they want to paint.

4 Have each child paint a picture of one of the places where the class walked.

5 Let the pictures dry and then have children cut them out. Place the pictures under a heavy flat object to minimize curling.

6 Write a caption using a preposition for each place on white construction paper. Example: *under the swings.* Cut around the words in a cloudlike shape. Write the title in the same manner.

7 Copy, enlarge, and cut out the footstep pattern here. Ask each child to trace and cut out five footsteps from red construction paper using the pattern.

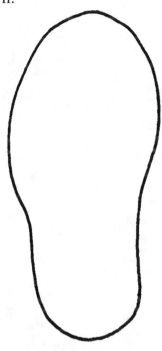

8 If you are using a class picture, staple it in one corner of the bulletin board. Make a caption to go with the picture that says: *Our class went on a long walk.*

9 Starting with the class picture, arrange the pictures and captions in the order that your class walked.

10 Staple the footsteps on the board to represent children's feet going over, under, and around.

Making the Class Big Book

Materials You Need

▲ two pieces of 22-by-28-inch poster board

▲ 18-by-24-inch tagboard

▲ rubber cement or white school glue

▲ black marker

▲ scissors

▲ hole punch

▲ long shoelace or cord

Here's What to Do

1 Cut the front and back covers from the poster board in the shape of a tennis shoe (as if you are looking down on the shoe).

2 As you are looking down on the shoe, draw its parts. Using the point of a scissors, punch small holes where the holes for the shoelaces would go.

3 String shoelaces or cords through the holes, making them crisscross the way a real shoe does. Tie a bow.

4 Glue the title on the front of the book.

5 Cut the inside pages out of tagboard to fit within the shoe-shaped covers.

6 Carefully remove the pictures, captions, and footsteps from the bulletin board.

7 Glue each picture with its caption on the inside pages using the front and back of each page. Glue the footsteps on each page to show the motions of going over, under, and around.

62

Extending Learning

◆ MATH

• Take the class outside and count the number of steps necessary to get from place to place.

• Help children measure the distance between different places in and around your school.

◆ PHYSICAL EDUCATION

Play a game of Giant Steps with the class on the playground or in the gym. Beforehand, teach children various steps including a giant step, a baby step, a ballet dancer step in which you twirl around, a hopping step, a sliding step, and any others you wish to add. Have children line up on one side of the playground. Explain that you will call out a name and specific instructions. For example: "Sara, you may take three baby steps." Sara must remember to say "May I?" before she takes her steps. If she forgets, she can't move or must return to the starting line. The object of the game is to reach you first. Play several practice rounds until children get the idea. Then allow them opportunities to give instructions.

◆ LANGUAGE ARTS

Play a guessing game using prepositions. Begin by writing some common prepositions on the board. Review these to be sure children know their meaning. Then explain how to play the game. For example, you might say, "I am thinking of something that is *on* my desk." See how many guesses it takes children to figure out what the object is. Once children get the idea, they can give the clue using different prepositions.

◆ LITERATURE LINKS

I Was Walking Down the Road by Sarah Barchas (Scholastic, 1975)

I Went Walking by Sue Williams (Harcourt Brace, 1977)

Lily Takes a Walk by Satoshi Kitamura (Dutton, 1987)

Rooster's Off to See the World by Eric Carle (Simon & Schuster, 1972)

Sitting in My Box

by Dee Lillegard
Dutton, 1989

With only his imagination for company, a little boy sits alone in a big cardboard box. He is soon joined by animal after animal with hilarious results.

Making the Bulletin Board

Materials You Need

▲ white construction paper

▲ tempera paint and paintbrushes

▲ cut-out letters for the title and the last caption

▲ scissors or X-acto knife

▲ a large carton such as a TV comes in (Save the entire box. You will need the front for the bulletin board and the book's front cover, and the back for the book's back cover.)

▲ pushpins

▲ stapler

Here's What to Do

1. Read the story to the class, emphasizing the rhyme and repetition. Encourage children to join in and predict what might happen next.

2. Ask: What other animals might come knocking on the box? Invite each child to think of one animal character to include in the story.

3. Have children paint their characters. Ask a volunteer to paint the child who is sitting in the box.

4. Let the pictures dry and then have children cut them out. Place them under a heavy object to prevent curling.

5. Cut off the front of the large box. Keep the top flap and three or four inches of cardboard on each side. Score the side pieces with scissors or an X-acto knife down the middle of each section. This makes it easier to fold the flaps in and out so that they then can be attached to the board. Pushpins work well to hold the box on the board.

6. Place the picture of the child so it appears in the middle of the box. Arrange the animal characters on the bulletin board to make them appear to be partially in the box or coming out of it. Let some of them overlap. Invite children to give each character a label, such as *a hairy gorilla knocks*.

7. Provide speech balloon patterns and ask children to write on them: *Let me, let me in*. Arrange these speech balloons around the animals to look as if the animals are talking.

8. Use cut-out letters for the title of the book and staple at the top of the board.

9. Under the box, use cut-out letters to say, *So we all moved over!*

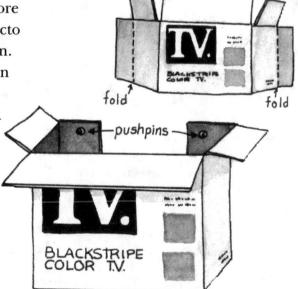

Making the Class Big Book

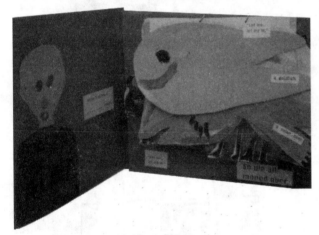

Materials You Need

▲ front and back of the large box used on the bulletin board

▲ construction paper or brown butcher paper cut into large squares

▲ scissors

▲ rubber cement or school glue

▲ cut-out title letters from the board

▲ metal O rings

Here's What to Do

1 Take the box down from the bulletin board and cut off the side flaps and the top flap. You need only a flat piece of cardboard for the cover. Cut an identical piece from the back of the box to be the back cover.

2 Glue the title letters from the bulletin board onto the front of the box.

3 This is a flip book. Each of the characters flips over and covers the previous one.

4 For the inside pages of the book, cut the construction paper or brown butcher paper for each child's page in a square about two-thirds the size of the cover.

5 Carefully remove the pictures and captions from the bulletin board.

6 Glue the picture of the child on the inside of the book cover. Write the words *Sitting in my box . . .*

7 Glue each picture with its label as well as one of the speech balloons on a page.

8 Glue the words *So we all moved over!* on the inside of the back cover at the bottom of the page. By putting the words at the bottom of the page, you are able to see the caption each time one of the characters is flipped over.

9 Punch two holes at the top of each animal and at the left sides of the front and back covers. Assemble the book using metal O rings.

NOTE: To read this book, make the front and back stand up at a right angle to each other. Flip all of the animals over the back of the back cover. As you are looking at the book, you can see the little child sitting on one side as you read "Sitting in my box." Then flip over the first animal and read its label; for example, *a hairy gorilla knocks.*

Extending Learning

◆ MATH

Count all of the animals that are in the original story and in the class story. Figure out the most and fewest legs in the box at one time.

◆ DRAMATIC PLAY

Provide a large cardboard box and invite children to use it to act out the story. Children might also make paper plate masks to represent the different animals that visit the box.

◆ LANGUAGE ARTS

As a variation of this story, use the names of children in the class instead of animals. Each child paints a picture of himself or herself, and the text reads, for example, *Tanya Smith came knocking.* This is a great activity for the beginning of the year as children are getting to know one another.

◆ LITERATURE LINKS

The Bus Ride by Nancy Jewell (Scott Foresman, 1976)

Dear Zoo by Rod Campbell (Puffin Books, 1982)

The Napping House by Audrey Wood (Harcourt Brace, 1984)

Zoo Doings by Jack Prelutsky (Trumpet Club, 1983)

Ten Black Dots

by Donald Crews
Greenwillow, 1986

What can you do with ten black dots? "One dot can make a sun or moon when the day is done. Two dots can make the eyes of a fox . . ." This imaginative counting book is told in simple rhymes that tell what dots can become.

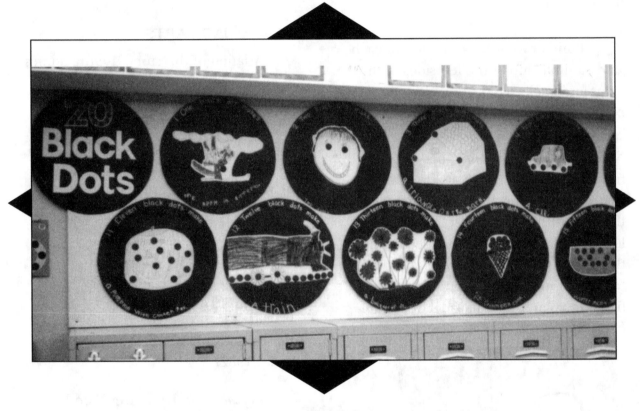

Making the Bulletin Board

Materials You Need

▲ white and black construction paper
▲ tempera paint and paintbrushes
▲ white cut-out letters for the title
▲ ³/₄-inch black dots (cut from black construction paper or gummed labels)

▲ construction paper scraps
▲ a class picture
▲ silver metallic marker
▲ black tagboard
▲ glue or rubber cement

Here's What to Do

1 Read the story to the class. Discuss how the dots are used on each page. Find circle-shaped items in your classroom. Brainstorm other ways dots could be part of a picture.

2 Decide how many dots you want to use in your bulletin board and class book. We had 20 children so we titled ours *20 Black Dots*. Sometimes children prefer to work in pairs, so we could have made a board and book called *10 Black Dots* with two children working on one page together. The nice thing about this book is that you can make as many pages as you like, and it is challenging enough for older children.

3 Assign each child a number and provide that many black dots. Invite children to use the dots to make a picture on white construction paper. Encourage the use of a variety of media—paint, crayons, colored pencils, construction paper scraps. Talk about the need for planning before gluing or sticking dots on the paper.

4 Let the pictures dry and have children cut them out. Glue each picture on a large circle cut from black construction paper.

5 Using a silver metallic marker, print the first half of the caption at the top of the black paper, following the curve of the paper (for example, *Two black dots make . . .*). Finish the caption at the bottom of the circle (for example, *. . . two eyes on a little girl*). Students in first or second grade can easily do all of this printing.

6 Use white cut-out letters for the title. We made the "20" out of red paper and glued on small black dots for an interesting effect. Glue all letters on one of the black circular shapes to make the title page. To save yourself some work later on, glue the letters of the title on a circular piece of black tagboard that will then serve as the cover of the class book.

7 The last black circle on the bulletin board contains the class picture. We enlarged our class picture and used cut-out letters to say *By 20 Bright Spots* to designate the authors of the book.

8 Arrange and staple the black dots on the bulletin board in numerical order.

Making the Class Big Book

Materials You Need

▲ black tagboard
▲ rubber cement or school glue
▲ cut-out letters for the title
▲ metal O rings

Here's What to Do

1. Carefully take the pages off the bulletin board using a staple remover so children's work doesn't get torn.

2. If you made the title page out of black tagboard (see step 6 in Making the Bulletin Board), your book cover is ready. You need to make only one more black tagboard circle for the back cover.

3. Sometimes children like to have a page that says "The End." If so, use white cut-out letters (to match the title) or print using the silver marker on another piece of black construction paper and put this page at the end. The author page with the class picture can be inserted after the title page or at the end of the book. Laminate the pages if desired.

4. Punch two holes at the left side of each page and assemble the book using metal O rings.

Extending Learning

◆ SCIENCE

Help children find dots or circles in nature. Possibilities include the sun, centers of flowers, fruits, and planets. Create a book or poster titled "Nature's Dots."

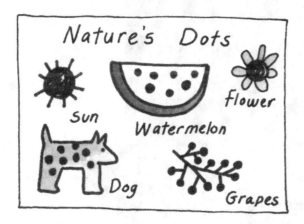

◆ MATH

This story lends itself well to recognition of numerals and allows children to practice rote counting. Older children will enjoy the challenge of counting all of the dots in the original text as well as in the class book they create.

◆ LANGUAGE ARTS & ART

Some children may enjoy writing a complete dot book of their own. Younger children may want to go up to only 5 while older children may enjoy the challenge of using larger numbers of dots.

◆ HOME-SCHOOL CONNECTION

With a hole punch, make lots of black dots. Place 20 or so dots in envelopes and give one to each child. Have children take these dots home to work with a family member to create different dot designs. Send along a note suggesting that they work on a piece of white paper.

◆ LITERATURE LINKS

Here are four great counting books that young children enjoy.

One Gorilla by Atsuko Morozumi (Farrar, Straus & Giroux, 1990)

One Hunter by Pat Hutchins (Greenwillow, 1982)

1, 2, 3 to the Zoo by Eric Carle (Putnam, 1990)

What Comes in 2's, 3's, & 4's? by Suzanne Aker (Scholastic, 1990)

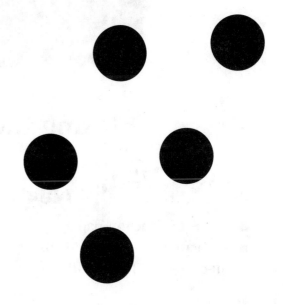

When the King Rides By

by Margaret Mahy
Scholastic, 1986

"Oh, what a fuss when the king rides by." A cumulative rhyme describes the increasing commotion that results as dogs and babies, cats and ladies, soldiers and mice all join the king's parade.

Making the Bulletin Board

Materials You Need

▲ white construction paper
▲ tempera paint and paintbrushes
▲ cut-out letters for the title

▲ scissors
▲ sentence strips
▲ markers
▲ optional: collage materials such as paper scraps, feathers, buttons

Here's What to Do

1 Read this story aloud with great flair so that children soon notice the text's rhyming and cumulative style. Encourage children to chime in on the refrain. Spend time talking about the characters.

2 Individually or in pairs, let children choose which stanza and characters they want to paint. After the pictures are finished, let them dry. As an option, children can add collage materials such as feathers for the pigeons.

3 Cut out the pictures after they are dry. Place them under a heavy flat object to minimize curling.

4 Write the captions for each stanza, as they appear in the book, on the sentence strips.

5 Arrange the pictures starting at the top of the board progressing down in a left to right order. The last picture is the refrain, *And the drum plays rat-a-tat-tat.*

Making the Class Big Book

WHEN THE
KING RIDES BY

written by Margaret Mahy
retold and illustrated by
Middle Kindergarten

Materials You Need

- ▲ two 14-by-18-inch pieces of colored poster board
- ▲ 12 pieces of 12-by-18-inch white tagboard
- ▲ 2-inch-wide clear packing tape
- ▲ rubber cement or white school glue
- ▲ cut-out letters for the title
- ▲ aluminum foil or metallic paper
- ▲ cotton
- ▲ scissors

Here's What to Do

1. This story works well as an accordion book. Cut each of the two pieces of poster board into a crown shape.

2. Cover these pieces with aluminum foil to represent the king's crown.

3. Pull and stretch cotton until it is a thin film of fluff. Glue it along the bottom of the crown.

4. Tape the inside pieces of 12-by-18-inch tagboard to each other so that they form a long line of pages. Leave about 1/8 inch of space between the pages so they can fold back and forth. Tape the front and back crowns at each end.

5. Glue the title letters on the king's crown.

6. Carefully remove the pictures and captions from the bulletin board.

7. Glue one picture with its captions on each page of tagboard. Be sure to put them in the same order as they appear in the story.

8 You can laminate the entire book in one long sheet or laminate each page before taping the pages together into one line.

9 Fold the pages back and forth to make an accordion book. When you display the book in your classroom, set it up on a table so that it makes the zigzag accordion pattern.

Extending Learning

◆ SOCIAL STUDIES

Find out if children know that a king is a ruler. Talk about names for other kinds of rulers, such as president, premier, czar, prince, princess, emperor, empress. Ask children to name some qualities that they think a good ruler should have.

◆ DRAMATIC PLAY

Hold a class parade to reenact the king's procession. Students might enjoy making simple props and costumes from paper or scrap materials. If possible, play marching music for the parade or invite students to make their own with drums and whistles.

◆ LANGUAGE ARTS

• Remind children that this book includes rhyming words. Have them pick out the words that rhyme. Then challenge them to think of other words that rhyme with these as well. Compile rhyming lists for children to use in their writing activities.

• Play I Spy and give clues for children to locate specific characters on each page. For example: "I spy a baby in a carriage wearing a bonnet." Encourage children to use descriptive phrases and clues for their classmates to guess.

◆ LITERATURE LINKS

Here are other books about royalty, told in a cumulative or repetitive manner.

Drummer Hoff by Barbara Emberley (Troll, 1967)

King Bidgood's in the Bathtub by Don and Audrey Wood (Harcourt Brace, 1985)

The King's Cat by John Tarlton (Scholastic, 1987)

May I Bring a Friend? by Beatrice Schenk DeRegniers (Atheneum, 1964)

Who Sank the Boat?

by Pamela Allen
Putnam, 1990

A cow, a donkey, a sheep, a pig, and a mouse decide to go rowing in a very small boat. As each climbs aboard, disaster grows more imminent. The story is funny, the pictures are splendid, and the easy text is just right for young readers.

Making the Bulletin Board

Materials You Need

- ▲ white construction paper
- ▲ tempera paint and paintbrushes
- ▲ cut-out letters for the title
- ▲ scissors
- ▲ stapler
- ▲ white school glue
- ▲ blue cellophane

- ▲ two pieces of 18-by-22-inch poster board (for the boat)
- ▲ one piece of 18-by-24-inch bulletin board paper (for the oar)
- ▲ pushpins and straight pins
- ▲ transparent tape
- ▲ optional: piece of rope approximately 6 feet long, 1-inch-thick dowel rod, and 2-by-12-inch piece of wood (for the dock)

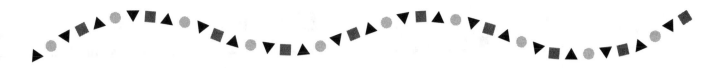

Here's What to Do

1 Read the story to the class. Draw children's attention to the rhyming text and the descriptions of the animals.

2 Encourage children to think of other animals or characters who could get into the boat. Help each child decide on one character to paint. Have children paint their pictures.

3 Let the pictures dry. Help children to cut them out. Place the dry paintings under a heavy flat object to minimize curling.

4 Make the boat in two pieces from the two pieces of 18-by-22-inch poster board. Cut out the front and back of the boat so that both sides are the same size and shape. Later, these will become the front and back covers of the class book.

5 If you are using rope, glue it to the top rim of the boat and leave 18 inches so the boat can be tied to the dock.

6 Attach the boat to the bulletin board using straight pins or staples.

7 Make the oar by rolling a piece of 18-by-24-inch bulletin board paper into a long tube and tape securely. Next, cut out a paddle shape. Cut two slits in the bottom of the tube and slide the paddle piece up into the slits. Use straight pins to attach the oar to the board.

8 To make the dock, attach the wooden board and dowel to the bulletin board by making a "shelf" of pushpins on which the wooden pieces can rest. Straight pins, inserted at angles, can also help stabilize the dock. Tie the boat to the dock with the rope.

9 Cut blue cellophane to look like waves and water. Staple it to the board at the bottom of the boat.

10 Arrange the animals to look as if some are in the boat, some are about to fall out of the boat, and others are just getting on the boat. Staples and straight pins allow the most flexibility in securing the animals to the board.

11 Make a caption for each character that says, *Was it the [animal's name]?* Attach the caption near the picture of the animal. If children want to choose one of the animals to be the one that sank the boat, you can randomly draw a name out of a hat. For that character the caption would say, for example, *It was the slimy lizard.*

12 Staple the title at the top of the board.

Making the Class Big Book

Materials You Need

▲ construction paper or bulletin board paper cut into the shape of one half of a boat

▲ rubber cement or white school glue

▲ scissors

▲ cut-out letters for the title

▲ metal O rings

Here's What to Do

1 The front and back covers of this book are made from the boat. Recall how you made the front half of the boat identical in size and shape with the back half of the boat (see step 4 in Making the Bulletin Board). If you glued rope along the top rim of the boat, cut it apart so you can separate the front and back pieces. Glue the title from the board on the front cover.

2 For the inside pages of the book, cut construction paper or bulletin board paper in the same size and shape as the front and back covers.

3 Carefully remove the pictures and captions from the bulletin board using a staple remover to avoid tearing children's work.

4 Glue each picture with its caption on the boat-shaped paper. Laminate the pages if desired.

5 Punch two or three holes at the side of each page and assemble the book using metal O rings or tie it together using some of the rope from the boat. Show children how the covers make an entire boat when they are completely open.

Extending Learning

◆ SCIENCE

Set up a sink-and-float learning center with a small tub of water. Provide a variety of objects for children to test to see if they sink or float. Record the results on a class chart.

◆ HEALTH AND SAFETY

Take this opportunity to review safety rules about swimming and using boats with the class. If possible, have the gym teacher or a local lifeguard come in to talk to children.

◆ MATH

Float jar lids of various sizes in a small tub of water. Let children experiment with adding pennies, one at a time, to see how many pennies it takes to sink each lid. Have children make predictions and estimations based on information gained.

◆ SOCIAL STUDIES

Help children find out about the different types of boats that people use (steamships, tugboats, rowboats, canoes, sailboats, etc.). Have resources on hand to show children pictures of what various boats look like. Two excellent resources are *What's Inside? Boats* (Dorling Kindersley, 1992) and *Amazing Boats* by Margarette Lincoln (Knopf, 1992).

◆ LANGUAGE ARTS

Encourage the children to innovate on the text and write their own versions of the story in mini-book form.

◆ LITERATURE LINKS

Mr. Archimedes' Bath by Pamela Allen (HarperCollins, 1982)

Mr. Grumpy's Outing by John Burningham (Macmillan, 1970)

"Pardon?" Said the Giraffe by Colin West (HarperCollins, 1986)

◆ Notes ◆